FOOTBALL
THE GOLDEN AGE

FOOTBALL
THE GOLDEN AGE

extraordinary images from 1900 to 1985

John Tennant

Bounty
Books

First published in Great Britain in
2001 by Cassell & Co

This edition published 2005 by Bounty Books,
an imprint of Octopus Publishing Group Ltd,
2-4 Heron Quays, London E14 4JP

Cassell & Co acknowledge the assistance
provided by Getty Images/Hulton Getty.

A CIP catalogue record for this book is
available from the British Library.

ISBN   0 7537 1072 2
ISBN 13 9780753710722

Printed and bound in Italy

FOREWORD

'Even now, whenever I arrive at any football ground, or merely pass close to one when it is silent, I experience a unique alerting of the senses. The moment evokes my past in an instantaneous emotional rapport which is more certain, more secret, than memory.'
'THE FOOTBALL MAN' BY ARTHUR HOPCRAFT

PHOTOGRAPHS OF THE 'DECISIVE MOMENTS' in football matches, particularly goals, are a staple of tomorrow's sports pages. Very soon after the points are won these action pictures lose their edge and are dull; their shelf-life is short. And any significance derives from their being proof of an important victory more than any intrinsic photographic merit.

So this collection of photographs is not about 'action'; there are no match-turning tricks or last-minute winners. It is concerned with things more romantic and idiosyncratic than just 'Goals On Camera': the seemingly inconsequential moments that every fan cherishes.

My dad took me to see the 1963 Cup Final. In spite of the excitement of the occasion, all memory of the match, its incidents, near misses, fouls and goals is hazy, distorted and somehow irrelevant. But nearly forty years later I still clearly remember fussing over which particular 'lucky' rosette to buy (I chose well). And the 'Orange Fruitie' I enjoyed on the bus after the game.

So that much of what fascinates me about football is an adjunct to the game itself. The thrill of a match encompasses more than the 90 minutes played out on the pitch: it embraces the sight and sound of the crowd and the journey to and from the ground. I have tried to capture the curiosity that is football — a mix of superstition, celebrity, science, devotion, humour and the plain ridiculous — in the photographs I have selected. Look at the automated ball-throwing machine on page 18 and the 'Tornado' boots on page 129. They may seem comical now but we do not know how kind time will be to the high-tech kit in use today — or to Adidas Predators.

It is not only football that has exploited technological advances. Photography began to take a firm hold in daily newspapers after World War I, and right up to the late Fifties it was usual for photographers covering football matches to shoot on plate cameras, with perhaps a maximum of ten frames for the entire game. Even in this time before the stranglehold of television, portraiture and other background stories were all tackled with the same economy. Today, motor-driven cameras are capable of squeezing off five frames a second.

Wherever possible, the photographs are attributed, although most of the old picture agencies operated on the basis that their names, not those of individual photographers, were credited. In the earliest images the 'unknown photographer' is well represented. Some names may be, deservedly, familiar: Bill Brandt, Bert Hardy, Kurt Hutton and Reg Speller, for example; and, more recently, Terry Fincher, Terry O'Neill, Kent Gavin, Ray Green and Monty Fresco.

Many of the images in this selection have been found in newspaper libraries — the 'Daily Herald', 'Daily Express' and 'Evening Standard' — and the 'Picture Post' archive. As well as at agency collections such as Fox, Keystone and Planet News.

The photographs have been chosen because they are arresting in their own right, not just because a player or club happened to achieve greatness. Some players, brilliant on the field but more reserved off it, may not be included. Others, more outgoing, appear more than once; clearly they enjoyed playing to the crowd and the camera. Similarly, the book looks beyond the polarised focus of the national press: the glamorous, successful sides (or those in difficulties) on one hand and a sideways regard for the 'giant-killing' underdog on the other.

As for the book's title, football may be said to have entered its 'golden age' around the beginning of the twentieth century. In 1905 Middlesborough paid Sunderland £1,000 for inside-forward Alf Common. And throughout the game, increasingly skilful players, combined with growing tactical awareness, were routinely attracting huge crowds.

Between then and now — most significantly — England won the World Cup in 1966, an event that has skewed our perception and expectations of football forever.

But perhaps what separates that burst of interest a hundred years ago – together with the great sides of the Twenties and Thirties and the swashbuckling teams and glamorous stars of the Fifties, Sixties and Seventies to which it gave rise – from the increasingly corporate entertainment we follow today is the common spirit that links the majority of the photographs in this book, which, if push became shove and led to a yellow card, may be defined as 'innocence'.

And if in the Eighties this 'golden age' ended, then it would only be fashionable to blame Big Business: TV, all-seater stadia, astronomical wage bills and the rise and rise of the ubiquitous agent. We have taken our sporting heroes and turned them into celebrities.

The difference between Stanley Matthews and David Beckham? A few million pounds a year and an excess of petulance. Stanley wore longer shorts and didn't marry a Spice Girl. And nobody except Stanley Matthews wore Stanley Matthew's shirt. But they share what matters — the gift: creating expectation every time the ball is at their feet. JOHN TENNANT

INTRODUCTION by Rodney Marsh

REMEMBER Terry O'Neill's photograph of 'The Clan' vividly [see pages 370–371]. We'd just enjoyed a slap-up lunch at a Fleet Street restaurant; the booze had been flowing and we were only too pleased to pose for Terry, who was a friend of mine and some of the others who were there. Even during the relaxed Seventies, this photograph, capturing as it does some of the cream of the nation's professional footballers, large cigars in hand and looking more like the cast of a Hollywood movie, was something of a coup for Terry.

Players from rival teams still socialise together, but you can imagine the reaction now if the shot was re-created with players from the top sides in the Premiership. I don't suppose Sir Alex would be too pleased if any of his lads were to appear in the press flanked by brandy glasses and smoking the finest Havanas Cuba has to offer. Now there's an idea...

Just as evocative are the photographs of the fans that appear in this amazing collection. When I was young, I'd be carried to Highbury on my dad's shoulders, and be part of the immense throng that crammed into the North Bank to watch Arsenal. Looking back now, it seems impossible that so many people could fit into grounds that now hold only half as many spectators.

And like most players, that's how I began my love affair with the game: as a supporter. From the age of six, I was kicking a ball around in the streets and dreaming of the day when I'd walk out at Wembley as captain of England. Johnny Haynes was my first hero, and the England captain of the time, but the book is packed with players to whom I looked up, even though some of them were playing at the same time as me.

Jimmy Greaves was probably the greatest goalscorer of all time, and someone whose ability impressed me so much that I actually spent time in training trying to finish like him – I couldn't. Then there was Bobby Moore, a friend and team-mate, and probably the game's first media superstar. He and his first wife Tina were the Posh and Becks of their time: glamorous, fashionable and idolised by people all over the nation. Then there's my old pal George Best, who, along with Pele, remains the most naturally gifted footballer I've ever seen. As the photos here testify, George was a phenomenally good-looking man, and he took over Bobby Moore's mantle as the most photographed British footballer and became an icon. I got to play alongside Bobby and George at Fulham [see right].

There are scores of other players in this book whom I watched and admired, either as a fan or a contemporary, but some of the most powerful images capture those who'd only be recognized by close family. These are the kids who have always been found – as I was – playing down any street, in any playground and on any patch of grass across the country; and the Sunday and lunch-break footballers who are still scoring that last-minute winner in the FA Cup Final.

This book offers many more insights into what the game means to people and its history. Some of the images captured here, such as the construction of Wembley's twin towers and the classic old East Stand at White Hart Lane, tell the story of football's previous boom, when, in the years after the first World War, new stadia sprang up everywhere. Only in the last five years or so has the game been able to afford a similar rebuilding programme, and I'm sure that in time we'll look back upon the 1990s and beyond as the start of another golden era.

But will these moments be captured in the same way? I doubt it.

Which is why we need a book like this one. It's not, as John says, about the goals, but about what makes the goals important: the charisma of the great players and managers, the passion of the fans, the fact that football will take you from one emotional extreme to the other. All in the space of 90 minutes, as any England fan can tell you. The images collected here bring all of this home, and they make for a unique look back at 85 years of the game.

Which brings me back to another Terry O'Neill photograph: this one was taken in 1972, a few months after 'The Clan' shot and not long after I'd moved from Queens Park Rangers to Manchester City [see page 370]. With top footballers today earning over £100,000 a week, their relationship with the press has changed: while players and press then were friends and drinking companions, nowadays the players feel constantly threatened and hassled. But Terry was able to take a fantastic photograph of myself alongside Geoff Hurst, Gordon Banks, Martin Chivers and a few other familiar faces. And sat right at the centre of it – just where he liked to be – with all eyes on him and every inch 'The Godfather', is my manager at the time, Malcolm Allison.

It's unlikely that photographs such as this one will be taken again. And I doubt you'll see another manager like Malcolm in a hurry. But that's what this book is all about: one-offs.

RODNEY MARSH

Sheffield Wednesday supporters. Circa
1940. Photographer not known

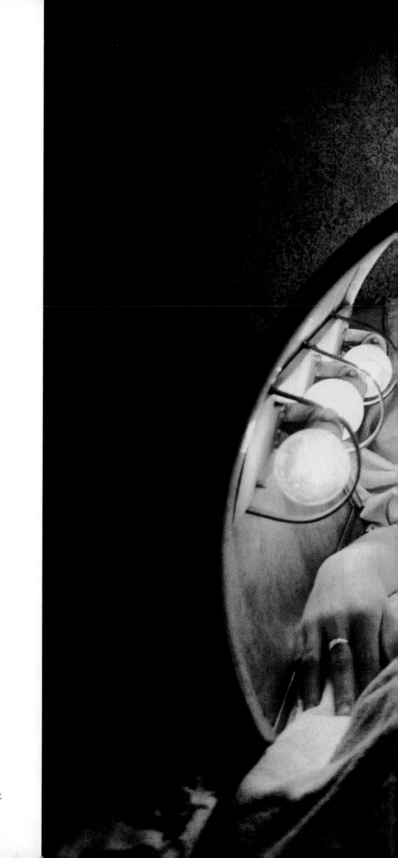

West Ham's full-back Jack Burkett undergoes heat-treatment
physiotherapy. January 1965. Photograph by Norman Quicke

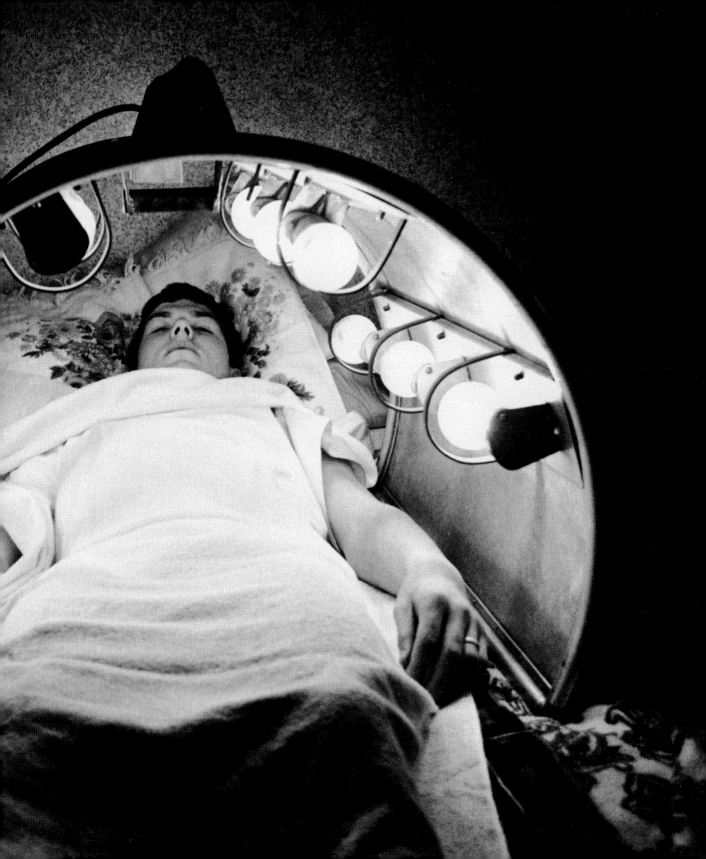

The annual Shrovetide football game
played at Ashbourne, Derbyshire.
March 1960. Photographer not known

Stanley Matthews and family on Blackpool beach.
September 1953. Photograph by Bert Hardy

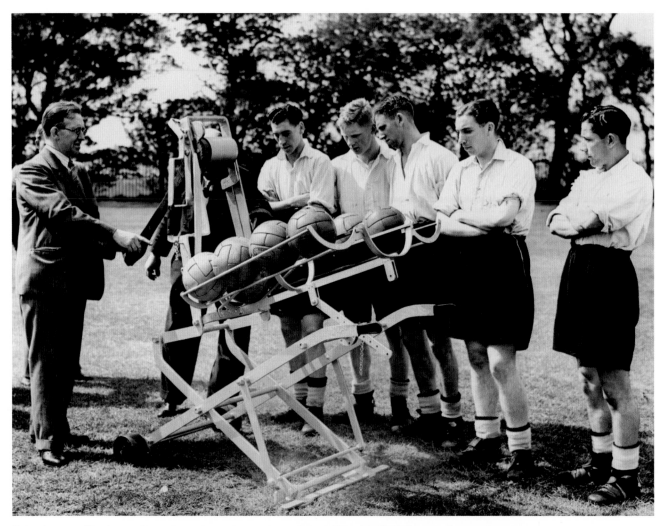

Wolverhampton Wanderers players inspect an automated crossing machine. July 1938. Photographer not known

Opposite: Watford goalkeeper Jim McLaren. January 1938. Photograph by E. Dean

Newpaper sellers on Victoria Embankment, London.
January 1936. Photograph by H.F. Davies

Barnsley equalise but Leicester City go on to win their FA Cup Sixth Round replay 2–1. March 1961. Photograph by Vic Clements

Southern League Yeovil Town beat Sunderland of Division One 2–1 in the Fourth Round of the FA Cup. January 1949. Photographer not known

Tommy Smith of Liverpool. February 1974.
Photograph by Bob Thomas

Opposite: Nobby Stiles of Manchester United.
November 1969. Photograph by Ray Green

Five hundred people watch the FA Cup Final on twenty television sets in Kensington Town Hall, London. Arsenal beat Liverpool 2–0. April 1950.
Photograph by E. Round

FIFA president Stanley Rous selects the type of ball to be used in the 1966 World Cup finals. May 1965. Photograph by Robert Stiggins

Opposite: Webbers, the London-based football manufacturer. December 1950. Photographer not known

Harry Rogers of Chalk Farm, London,
makes a promise to his customers. But
Chelsea go out 1–0 at home to Grimsby in
the Sixth Round of the FA Cup. 1939.
Photographer not known

Tottenham Hotspur take a preventative gargle against 'flu. January 1933. Photograph by E.E. Haynes

Wolverhampton Wanderers drink malted milk. April 1939. Photograph by Kurt Hutton

The Graf Zeppelin sails over Wembley during the FA Cup Final. Down on the pitch Arsenal beat Huddersfield 2–0. April 1930. Photograph by J. Gaiger. Opposite: photographer not known

Factory workers in
Kilmarnock, Scotland.
October 1955.
Photograph by
Malcolm Dunbar

Sunderland's £100,000 sextet: centre-half Roy Daniel, centre-forward Ted Purdon, outside-right Tom Wright, inside-forward Kenneth Chisholm, left-back William Elliott and outside-right Billy Bingham. February 1954. Photograph by M. Mckeown

Police remove boots and shoes from supporters when Manchester United visit Queens Park Rangers at Loftus Road. September 1975. Photographer not known

Opposite: A ticket tout outside Craven Cottage. February 1958.
Photographer not known

An England squad in club colours. Back row, left to right: Ray Wilson, Everton; Gordon Milne, Liverpool; George Cohen, Fulham; Willie Stevenson, Liverpool; Ron Springett, Sheffield Wednesday; Gordon Banks, Leicester City; Jack Charlton, Leeds United; Geoff Hurst, West Ham United; Peter Thompson, Liverpool; Paul Reaney, Leeds United; Gordon Harris, Burnley; Harold Shepherdson, England trainer.

Front row, left to right: Nobby Stiles, Manchester United; Norman Hunter, Leeds United; Keith Newton, Blackburn Rovers; Joe Baker, Arsenal; Alan Ball, Blackpool; Bobby Moore, West Ham United; Jimmy Greaves, Tottenham Hotspur; George Eastham, Arsenal; Ron Flowers, Wolverhampton Wanderers; Bobby Charlton, Manchester United. Spring 1966. Photographer not known

Littlewood pools winners. 1930s. Photographers not known

Ipswich Town players after a 2–1
defeat at home to Aston Villa in
their Third Round FA Cup replay.
January 1939. Photographer not
known

Preceding pages: A downpour at
Craven Cottage. 1965.
Photographer not known

Portsmouth supporter. April 1934. Photographer not known

Opposite: West Bromwich Albion supporter. April 1935.
Photograph by S.C. Smith

A British Army XI plays
an international team,
comprising two Belgians,
two Dutchmen, two Poles,
two Norwegians and
three Czechoslovakians,
at Stamford Bridge.
March 1941. Photograph
by Bert Hardy

Bobby Moore after West Ham United win the FA Cup Final. May 1964. Photograph by Kent Gavin
Opposite: Modelling Hardy Amies for a 'Daily Express' fashion shoot. 1966. Photograph by M. McKeown

Houses in Paxton Road are demolished to make way for a new stand at White Hart Lane. May 1936. Photograph by Martin

Opposite: The Clock End, Highbury. August 1930. Photographer not known

Pupils of St Joseph's College train with professional coach George Smith. October 1948. Photographs by George Konig

Edward, Prince of Wales, kicks off a friendly between Tottenham Hotspur and Fulham after inspecting the Champion Cadet Battalion at Sandhurst. 1921. Photographer not known

Opposite: The start of the Restaurant Junior Charity Cup Final at Highbury. April 1929. Photograph by Puttnam

Frank Swift,
Manchester City's
goalkeeper, also
works as a public
relations officer
for a catering firm.
January 1948.
Photograph by
Charles Hewitt

Chelsea training before their Sixth Round FA Cup tie against Liverpool. February 1932. Photographer not known

Wrexham training in the run-up to their Fourth Round FA Cup tie against Manchester United. January 1957. Photographer not known

West Ham United supporters
arrive at Wembley for the first
FA Cup Final to be played at the
national stadium; their team
loses 2–0 to Bolton Wanderers in
front of an estimated crown of
200,000. April 1923. Photographer
not known

Frankie Vaughan leads the singing at Wembley before the FA Cup Final between Leeds United and Sunderland. May 1973. Photographer not known

Opposite: FA Cup Final crowd control at Wembley for Arsenal versus Sheffield United. April 1936. Photographer not known

Bob Paisley in Liverpool's sponsor's colours at Anfield. May 1982. Photographer not known

Opposite: Leaving the pitch with the Division One Championship trophy after his last home game in charge of Liverpool. May 1983. Photographer not known

Kickabout, Purley Way, London. January 1969.
Photographer not known

Opposite: Torquay United train on the beach at Anstey's Cove.
February 1938. Photograph by Reg Speller

Overleaf, left: Plymouth Argyle supporters. January 1922.
Photographer not known

Overleaf, right: Arsenal supporters. February 1936.
Photograph by Hudson

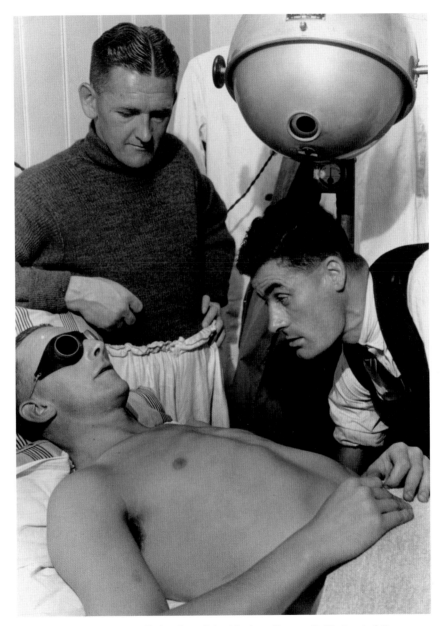

Johnny O'Harte looks on as Chelsea's assistant trainer, Norman Smith, treats fellow full-back Jacky Smith. August 1939. Photograph by Kurt Hutton

Opposite: Buxton Town's centre-half, Joe Wilson, enjoys a high-pressure shower massage. December 1951. Photograph by Hicklin

Leeds United's Electronic Summation System, on which the attendance in each part of Elland Road is recorded. 1950s.
Photographer not known

Workmen assemble seating at Wembley in last-minute preparation for the World Cup finals. July 1966. Photograph by Chris Barham

Goldie the golden eagle,
escapee from London Zoo,
perches in Regent's Park.
December 1965.
Photographer not known

Bolton Wanderers are on their way to Wembley for
the FA Cup Final against Manchester City. April 1926.
Photographer not known

Maldon Ladies Football Club, formed for a charity match, walk out for their ninety-fifth game. November 1953. Photograph by Peter Waugh

Opposite: Brenda Chittenden, goalkeeper for East Kent Packers. November 1953. Photographer not known

Walsall secretary Ernest Wilson entertains the crowd at Fellows Park. December 1952. Photograph by R. Saidman

Opposite: The Remote Control Telesonic Apparatus makes one-to-one coaching possible. January 1949. Photographer not known

West Ham United supporters at an
FA Cup Semi-final against Everton; their
team loses 2–1. March 1933. Photographer
not known

George Best is carried off injured. March 1969. Photographer not known

Opposite: In the bath at Old Trafford. 1967. Photograph by Ray Green

Warren Mitchell, as Alf Garnett, at Upton Park. February 1968. Photographer not known

Opposite: Wolverhampton Wanderers supporter. March 1949. Photograph by Charles Hewitt

The Arsenal squad trains
on the A6. July 1962.
Photographer not known

Preceding pages: The
home dressing-room at
Highbury. November 1938.
Photograph by H.F. Davies

Walthamstow Schoolboys after beating West Ham Schoolboys 3–1. January 1931. Photograph by A.R. Coster

Kickabout in London. 1962. Photographer not known

The Crazy Gang act as stretcher bearers at the
annual charity match between boxers and jockeys;
this year's game is played at The Den. October 1936.
Photograph by Ward

Colchester United play Norwich City. October 1950. Photograph by John Chillingworth

Opposite: The Colchester supporters' registration hut. October 1950. Photograph by M. McKeown

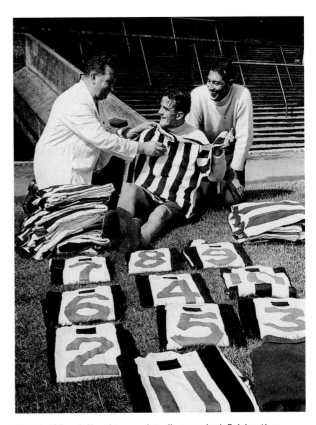

Wing half Frank Houghton and goalkeeper Jack Fairbrother with the Newcastle United's trainer Norman Smith. August 1948.
Photographer not known

Opposite: Portsmouth's kit-man Bill Wright. December 1952.
Photograph by R. Saidman

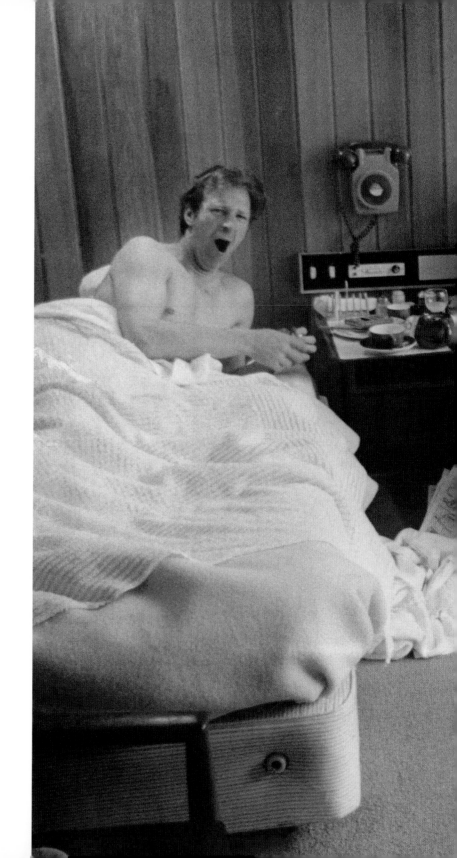

Jack Charlton and Billy Bremner share a room
for a Leeds United away game. May 1972.
Photograph by Henson

Tottenham Hotspur supporters protest the allocation of FA Cup Final tickets in Trafalgar Square. Spurs and Burnley are to receive 15,000 tickets each. April 1962. Photographer not known

Opposite: Wembley box office staff load tickets for posting. March 1945. Photographer not known

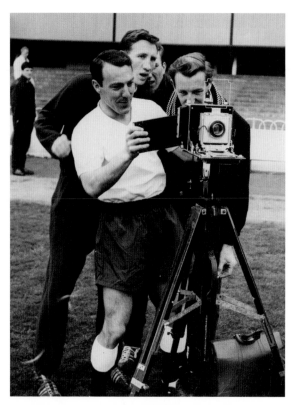

Jimmy Greaves at a Tottenham Hotspur photo-call.
April 1962. Photographer not known

Opposite: Centre half Sidney Plackett at a Notts County
photo-call. August 1929. Potographer not known

Kickabout, Salford. May 1955. Photograph by Salt

Kickabout, London. August 1933. Photographer not known

Three thousand bales of straw are laid at White Hart Lane to protect the pitch from frost. December 1925. Photograph by Davis

Opposite: Ground staff at Stoke City attempt to thaw the ground. Stanley Matthews warms his hands over one of the braziers. December 1938. Photographer not known

Fulham and Blackpool players observe two minutes' silence for King George V before the Fourth Round FA Cup tie at Craven Cottage. January 1936. Photographer not known

Opposite: A minute's silence for President Kennedy before Fulham play Sheffield United. November 1963. Photograph by Douglas Miller

Fred Packham, plater and polisher, on the day before the FA Cup Final. The cup is lifted by Roy Paul, captain of the Manchester City team that beats Birmingham City 3–1. May 1956. Photograph by Douglas Miller

Opposite: D. Wiseman and R.H. Brough draw Millwall at home to Tottenham Hotspur in the Third Round of the FA Cup. January 1967. Photographer not known

Nigeria's inside forward Ebenezer prepares for a match against
Bishop Auckland during his country's goodwill tour of Britain. 1950.
Photograph by Charles Hewitt

Opposite: The Nigeria team wear support straps but not boots.
Photograph by Charles Hewitt

Following page: Sheffield United supporters in the Mall before
the FA Cup Final. April 1936. Photograph by Allen

Tommy Docherty takes Chelsea on holiday to Cannes after winning the Second Division Championship. July 1963. Photographer not known

Following page: Cardiff City versus Chelsea at Ninian Park. March 1921. Photograph by Arthur R. Coster

Alf Ramsey prevents George Cohen from swapping shirts after England beat Argentina in the Quarter-final of the World Cup. July 1966.
Photographer not known

Preceding page, left: Arsenal's centre-forward Ted Drake dons a shinpad. January 1938.
Photographer not known

Preceding page, right: The 'Tornado', designed by former referee Englebert K. Harmer of Vienna, who explains 'The boot has no laces but is held fast to the foot by a rubber strap with rings on both sides of the heel. It is much lighter than a conventional boot and has a rubber padded instep with a "Special Kicking Pad" just beneath.' March 1958.
Photographer not known

Wembley ground staff prepare the flagpole before the first
FA Cup Final. The national stadium had taken 300 days to
build and was completed four days before the Final. April 1923.
Photographer not known

Opposite: One of Wembley's 'twin towers' under construction.
1923. Photographer not known

Tottenham Hotspur players take a brine bath at
Southend-on-Sea. January 1936. Photograph by Allen

Opposite: Centre-forward Jack Rowley of Manchester
United. February 1948. Photograph by William Vanderson

Half-back Arthur Grimsdell of Tottenham Hotspur parades the FA Cup, won with a 1–0 victory over Wolverhampton Wanderers (the Final was played at Stamford Bridge), down the High Road. April 1921. Photographer not known

Opposite: Spurs return the FA Cup to Football Association headquarters. February 1963. Photograph by Reg Lancaster

Chelsea goalkeeper Harry Medhurst coaching at Beverley School, New Malden, London. October 1949. Photographer not known

Opposite: Ten-year-old Billy Neil of Glasgow emigrating to Australia. October 1947. Photograph by Graham Hales

Littlewoods pools winner Keith Nicholson of Castleford, Yorkshire, is presented with a cheque for £152,319 by Bruce Forsyth. September 1961. Photograph by Ron Case

Opposite: Viv Nicholson, recently separated from husband Keith, with her £2,500 Chevrolet Impala. March 1962. Photographer not known

Bolton Wanderers players with Roy Pilkington, who has walked 195 miles from Bolton to Wembley to watch his team play Manchester United in the FA Cup Final. May 1958. Photographer not known

Opposite: Nottingham Forest return home with the FA Cup having beaten Luton Town 2–1. May 1959. Photographer not known

Brentford manager Jackie Gibbons commentates
for blind supporters, who are admitted free and
provided with headphones by the club. August 1951.
Photographer not known

Cardiff City's Len Davis demonstrates his reach. 1921.
Photographer not known

Opposite: Chlesea's new signing, Alex Stepney, watches his goalkeeping rival, Peter Bonetti, in training. August 1966.
Photographer not known

Spectators at Crystal Palace. April 1914.
Photographer not known

Everton supporters model 'weather–beaters' in the club's colours before the FA
Cup Final against West Bromwich Albion. May 1968. Photographer not known

Opposite: Bristol Rovers supporters. February 1958. Photograph by Terry Fincher

Newly developed plastic footballs are claimed
to be tougher than the traditional leather
ball. April 1952. Photographer not known

Constructing covered terracing
at The Valley. February 1934.
Photograph by Reg Speller

A ball-propelling machine tests centre-forwards, defenders and goalkeepers at Highbury. January 1950. Photographer not known

Stan Lynn of Birmingham City works on his shooting skills. January 1965. Photograph by R. Viner

A cameraman at Wembley films the FA Cup Final between
Sheffield Wednesday and West Bromwich Albion. April 1935.
Photographer not known

Opposite: Gaumont British Picture Corporation film schoolboy
football for a newsreel. April 1935. Photograph by Harry Todd

Deaf-and-dumb players from England and Wales
toss up. The Wales captain calls 'heads'. September 1925.
Photograph by Brooke

**Opposite: Arsenal versus Manchester United at Highbury.
January 1926.** Photograph by H.F. Davis

Hornsey YMCA on the rooftop of their clubhouse. September 1936.
Photograph by Fred Morley

Opposite: Saint Joseph's Academy, Blackheath, take down the goalposts after a game. February 1957. Photograph not known

Following pages: Hackney Marshes, London. October 1962.
Photographer not known

Left-half Wilf Copping of Arsenal. August 1934. Photograph by Fred Morley
Opposite: Goalkeeper Nigel Sims of Wolverhampton Wanderers. November 1952. Photograph by Charles Hewitt

The cast of 'Cuckoo in the Nest' backstage
at the Aldwych Theatre, London.
December 1925. Photographer not known

Kickabout in an empty dry dock at the Royal Albert Docks, London.
April 1931. Photographer not known

Opposite: Break time kickabout beneath the bows of the QE2, nearing
completion at the John Brown shipyard, Clydebank. September 1967.
Photographer not known

Norman Wisdom introduces the new club song to the crowd at Brighton and Hove Albion's Goldstone Ground. March 1965. Photographer not known

Opposite: Non-league Peterborough United, the night before their Second Round FA Cup tie against Swindon Town of Division Three South, visit the Prince of Wales Theatre, London, where they meet Ilona Adams and Tommy Cooper. December 1955. Photographer not known

Plymouth Argyle fans release their lucky balloon before a First Round
FA Cup tie against Notts County. January 1923. Photographer not known

Arsenal supporters at Highbury.
December 1951. Photograph by
George Douglas

Wounded soldiers at Blenheim Palace. 1916. Photographer not known

Disabled ex-servicemen attend a garden party at Buckingham Palace. July 1953. Photographer not known

Terry Venables at Stamford Bridge after being
dropped from the Chelsea team. April 1965.
Photograph by David Cairns

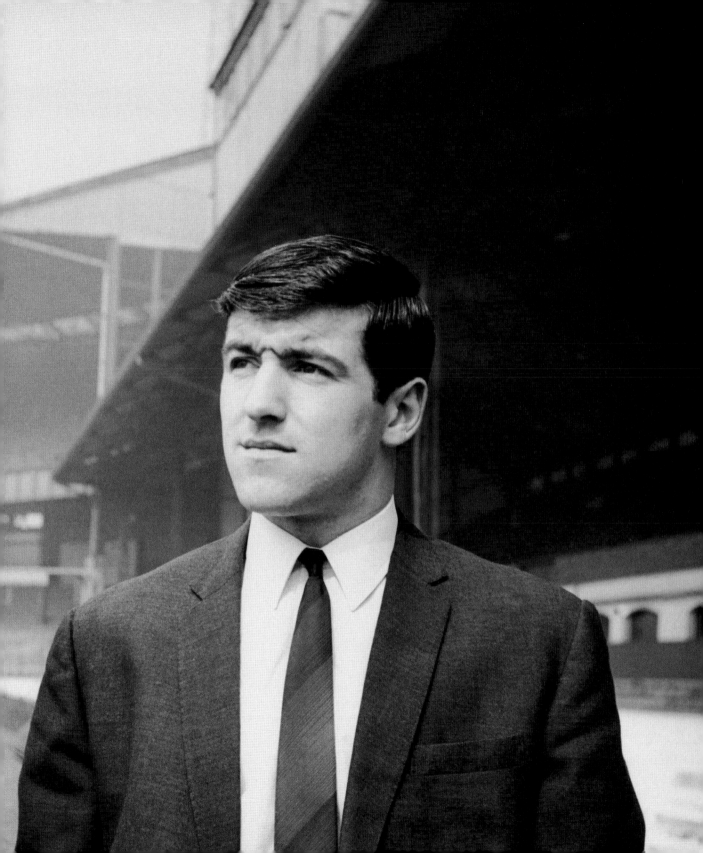

The Boleyn Ground, Upton
Park. March 1930.
Photograph by S.R. Gaiger

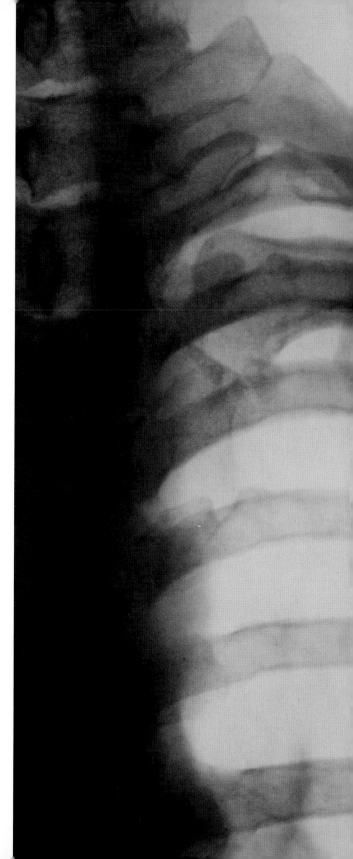

Bolton Wanderers' Nat Lofthouse recuperates with his family
following an operation on an injury picked up while playing
Tottenham Hotspur. March 1958. Photographer not known

Opposite: An X-ray of Lofthouse's shoulder after surgery.

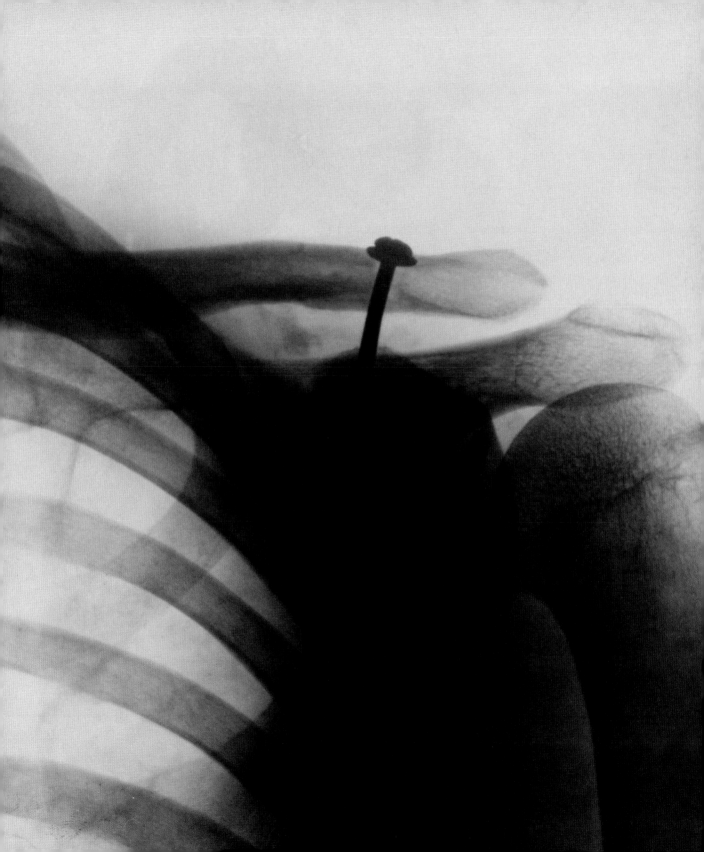

Captain and centre-half Jimmy Seddon, goalkeeper Dick Pym and centre-forward Harry Blackmore of Bolton Wanderers, the day after they beat Portsmouth 2–0 in the FA Cup Final. April 1929. Photographer not known

Bolton Wanderers manager Bill Ridding holds the FA Cup as Nat Lofthouse, captain of the side that beat Manchester United 2–0, takes a celebratory drink. May 1958. Photographer not known

The Tottenham cockerel is cleaned while White Hart Lane is enlarged, adding 25,000 to the capacity. July 1934. Photograph by R. Wesley

Opposite: The new stand under construction. July 1934. Photograph by H.F. Davis

Preceding pages: Arsenal supporters at
Highbury. December 1951. Photograph by
George Douglas

The annual mud-football game at the Leigh-on-
Sea regatta. August 1925. Photograph by Brooke

Cliff Bastin, who scored 150 League goals for Arsenal,
at home in Edgware after retiring from the game. 1948.
Photographer not known

Manager Bob Stokoe and captain Bobby Kerr, after Sunderland's 1–0 victory over Leeds United in the FA Cup Final. May 1973. Photograph by Douglas Miller

Opposite: An Everton supporter grabs the FA Cup from left winger Derek Temple, who scored the winner against Sheffield Wednesday. May 1966. Photographer not known

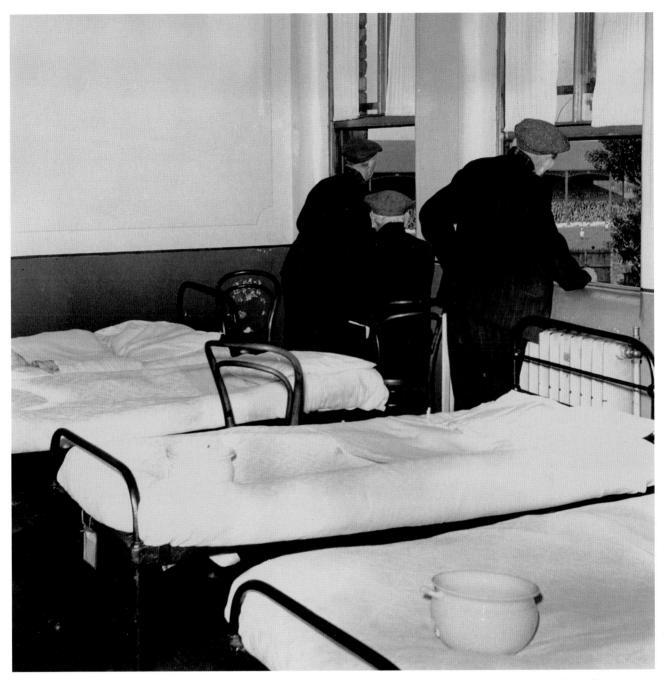

Pensioners watch a game at Ayresome Park from the windows of their hostel. November 1951. Photograph by George Douglas

Opposite: A lockout at Carrow Road for Norwich City's game against Portsmouth. January 1950. Photograph by F. Greaves

Spurs parade through Tottenham after beating Burnley 3–1 in the FA Cup Final. May 1962. Photograph by Douglas Miller

Opposite: On the open-top bus, Spurs players' sons Stephen Smith and Richard Blanchflower hold the cup. May 1962. Photographer not known

A Grimsby Town supporter waves a lucky cod mascot as
the team run out. March 1939. Photograph by David Savill

Alf Ramsey meets managers of northern teams. Back row, left to right: Trevor Porteous, player–manager of Stockport County; Les MacDowall, Oldham Athletic; Ronnie Suart, Blackpool; Harry Potts, Burnley; Jimmy Milne, Preston North End; Matt Busby, Manchester United; Harry Catterick, Everton; Don Revie, Leeds United; George Poyser, Manchester City;

Johnny Harris, Sheffield United. Front row, left to right: Stan Whitehorn, Football Association; Ike Robinson, Football Association; Alf Ramsey; Alan Brown, Sheffield Wednesday; Jack Marshall, Blackburn; John Carey, Nottingham Forest; Dave Russell, Tranmere Rovers. October 1964. Photographer not known

A Sunday washout in Essex. September 1926.
Photograph by H.F. Davis

Jackie Charlton on the pitch at Elland Road, where the ice is two inches thick. Leeds United say there is a '50-50' chance the cup-tie against Stoke can be played, but the match is eventually postponed for two months. January 1963. Photographer not known

Opposite: Liverpool's Kevin Keegan and Leeds United's Billy Bremner are sent off for fighting during the Charity Shield match at Wembley. August 1974. Photograph by Robert Stiggins

Preceding page, left:
Programme seller
at Stamford Bridge.
February 1949.
Photograph by
Chris Ware

Preceding page,
right: Wolverhampton
Wanderers fans
locked out of the FA
Cup semi-final replay
against Manchester
United at Goodison
Park. April 1949.
Photograph by
Charles Hewitt

Bobby and Tina
Moore, Epping
Forest. March 1966.
Photograph by
Terry O'Neill

Ticketless Newcastle United supporters outside Wembley while their team play – and lose to –
Liverpool in the FA Cup Final. May 1974. Photograph by Bart Leddy

A Manchester United supporter climbs into Wembley for the European Cup Final against Benfica.
May 1968. Photograph by Ron Case

Ballet teacher Yvonne Burr takes Ronald Peters,
captain of Littlehampton Boys' Club, through his positions.
The team win their first game after the new training 17-0.
1955. Photographer not known

Arsenal players leave for Germany to play against service teams. August 1945. Photographer not known

Army sergeants Joe Mercer of Everton, Matt Busby of Liverpool and Don Welsh of Charlton Athletic. 1939. Photographer not known

FA Cup holders Wolverhampton
Wanderers take the trophy
to their Third Round tie at
Plymouth Argyle. January 1950.
Photographer not known

221

The boot-room at Charlton Athletic. August 1936. Photograph by A. Hudson

Opposite: Collecting kit for the laundry at Highbury. October 1947. Photographer not known

Supporters queue for tickets to see Arsenal
play a friendly against Dynamo Moscow at White
Hart Lane. Highbury is still requisitioned for Air
Raid Precaution work. May 1945. Photograph by
William Vanderson

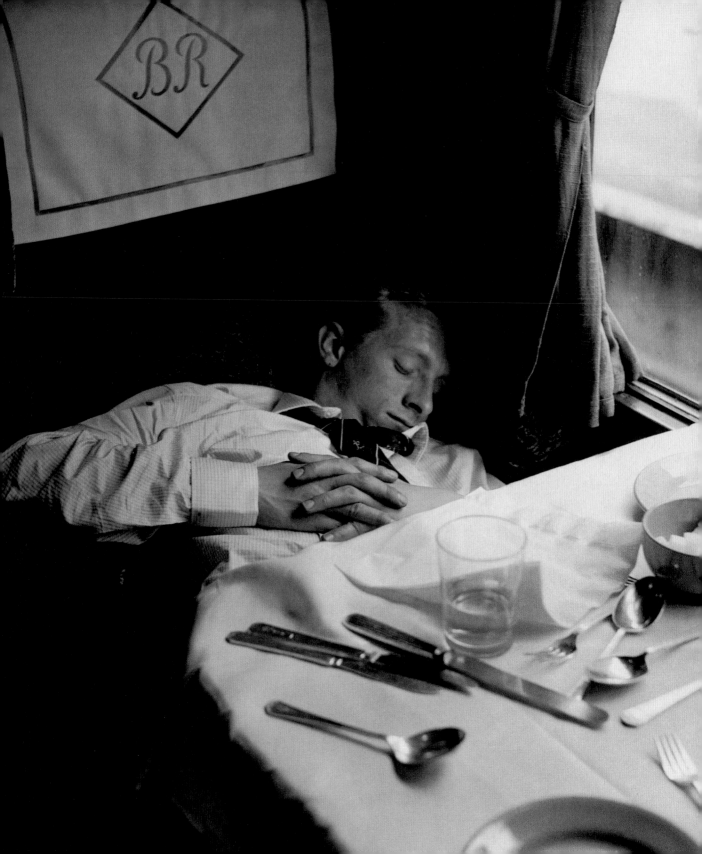

A supporter with Denis Law after Scotland beat England 3–2 at Wembley. The Scots are the first team to defeat Alf Ramsey's side since they won the World Cup the previous year. April 1967. Photographer not known

Opposite: Law asleep on the train home after Manchester United beat Leicester City 3–1 to win the FA Cup. May 1963. Photographer not known

Street game, London.
April 1950.
Photograph by Bill Brandt

Amos the donkey, Barnsley's mascot. 1910. Photographer not known

Opposite: A Notts County supporter at their First Round FA Cup tie away
to Queens Park Rangers. January 1923. Photographer not known

Manchester City take high tea with the Lord Mayor at the Town Hall, having beaten Portsmouth 2–1 to win the FA Cup. May 1934.
Photographer not known

West Ham United's manager Ron Greenwood takes the FA Cup back to Upton Park on the underground. He and the team have been up to London's West End to watch a cinema screening of highlights of their victory over Preston North End. May 1964.
Photographer not known

Preceding pages: A wreath is placed on board the plane bringing home the victims of the Munich aircrash. February 1958.
Photographer not known

England and Wolverhampton Wanderers captain Billy Wright with his landlady, Mrs Colley. 1950.
Photographer not known

Opposite: Arriving home from the 1958 World Cup to be met by Joy (his fiancée), Babs and Teddy
of the Beverley Sisters. June 1958. Photographer not known

Chelsea coach Dave Sexton demonstrates tactics during pre-season training. July 1963.
Photographer not known

Opposite: Leicester City players take lunch together at the club twice a week to help boost
team spirit. March 1949. Photograph by W. Jones

Arsenal parade the FA Cup outside
Islington Town Hall after beating
Huddersfield 2–0 in the final. April 1930.
Photographer not known

Middlesbrough's inside-forward Wilf Mannion in training. August 1952. Photographer not known

Opposite: Centre-forward Don Revie, suspended by Manchester City for missing training, keeps himself fit in a local park. August 1955. Photographer not known

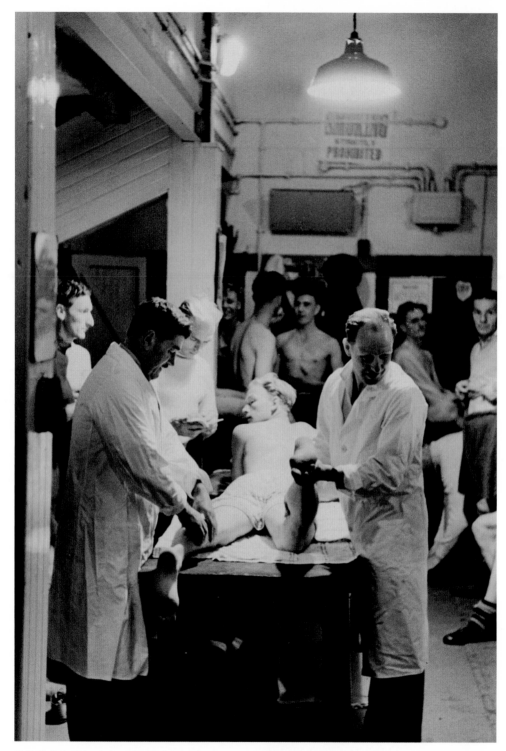

Hull City's half-back Jim Greenhaigh on the treatment table. August 1948. Photograph by Charles Hewitt

Opposite: Manchester City trainer Laurie Barnett with half-back Billy Walsh and inside-forward Spencer Evans in the dressing-room at Maine Road. February 1951. Photograph by John Chillingworth

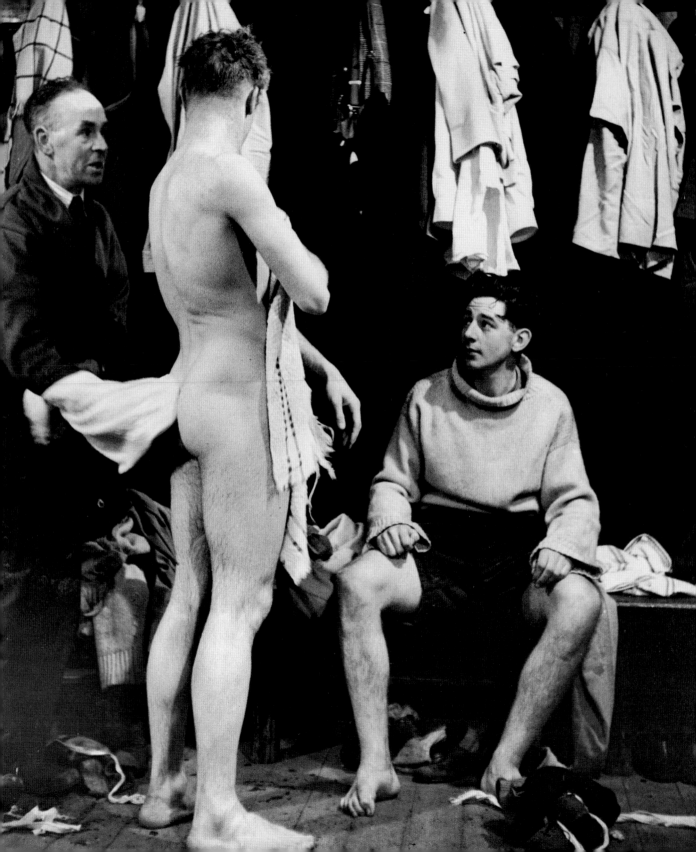

The Queen demonstrates her skill at table football during a visit to the British Industries Fair at Olympia, London. May 1955. Photographer not known

Opposite: Cissie Charlton arrives at Kings Cross station, London, on the way to see her sons Bobby and Jackie play against West Germany in the World Cup Final. July 1966. Photographer not known

Willie Waddell, Glasgow Rangers' right winger, at home with his son. 1950s. Photographer not known

Ally McLeod, Hibernian's left winger, at home with his dog. January 1962. Photographer not known

Blackpool supporters in London to see their team play Fulham in the Sixth Round of the FA Cup. February 1948. Photographer not known

Opposite: 'Ye Silent Twins': Manchester City supporters wear the outfits that won them first prize at Blackpool carnival. They are in London for the FA Cup Final against Bolton Wanderers. April 1926. Photograph by H. F. Davis

Joe Fagan in Rome with the European Cup, the morning after Liverpool beat Roma 4–2 on penalties. May 1984. Photograph by John Dawes

The annual football game
played in Atherstone,
Warwickshire. February 1914.
Photographer not known

Tottenham Hotspur before a charity match against a Variety Artists team. March 1923. Photographer not known

The Germany team before they play England in a friendly at White Hart Lane. England win 3–0. December 1935. Photographer not known

Chelsea manager Dave Sexton outside Stamford Bridge. October 1967. Photographer not known

Opposite: West Ham United defender Ken Brown and Chelsea midfielder Terry Venables visit Banham Road in Dagenham, where both were born. January 1965. Photograph by Norman Quicke

British architects, Ian Fraser, Ray Crownshaw and John Roberts with their design for a football
stadium commissioned by the Saudi Arabian royal family. September 1976. Photograph by Roger Jackson

Opposite: The finishing touches are put to the 80lb cake made to celebrate Southampton's
fiftieth anniversary. November 1935. Photograph by E. Philips

Ernie Allan, sales manager of stamp dealers Stanley Gibbons, takes delivery of the Jules Rimet trophy at Central Hall, Westminster, London, where it will be displayed at the National Stamp Exhibition. March 1966. Photographer not known

Opposite: Pickles, the dog who found the World Cup, while out for his bedtime walk in Norwood, London, after it had been stolen from the National Stamp Exhibition. March 1966. Photographer not known

Everton supporters arrive at Euston station; they are on the way to see their team play Arsenal at Highbury in a Fourth Round FA Cup tie. Arsenal win 4–3. January 1928. Photograph by H. F. Davis

Following pages: Supporters rush to the White Hart Lane box office to buy tickets to see Tottenham Hotspur against Glasgow Rangers in the Second Round of the European Cup Winners Cup. October 1962. Photograph by Tony Eyles

Above and opposite: Annual Shrovetide football match, Ashbourne, Derbyshire.
March 1952. Photographs by Bert Hardy

An Old Boys game at Harrow public school. October 1919. Photograph by Roper

Luton Town supporters on the way to their FA Cup Final against Nottingham Forest. May 1959. Photographer not known

Paul McCartney arrives at Wembley to see Everton play West Bromwich Albion in the FA Cup Final. May 1968. Photographer not known

Opposite: Rod Stewart on the terraces to see Scotland versus England at Hampden Park. May 1974. Photograph by D. Morrison

Rod Stewart leaves Hampden
Park after watching Scotland
beat England 2-0 in the Home
Championship. May 1974.
Photograph by D. Morrison

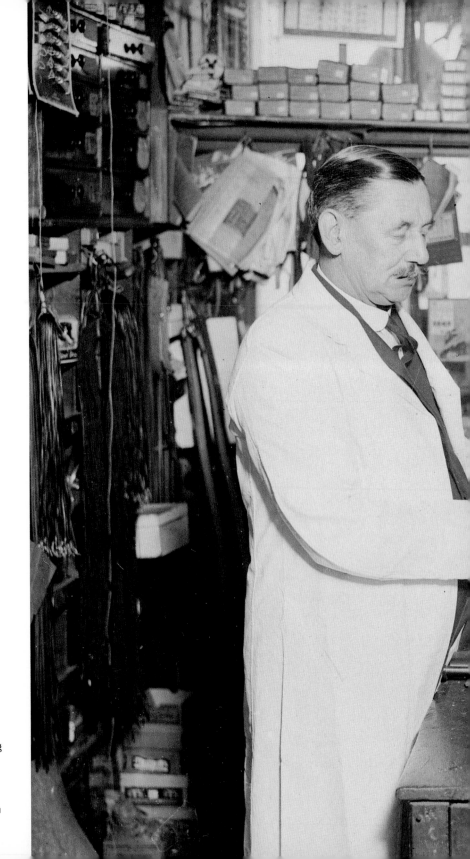

Preceding pages: Leytonstone after beating
local rivals Clapton Orient. May 1919.
Photograph by Nichols

Former Watford goalkeeper Bert Higgins
now owns a gentlemens' outfitters.
February 1932. Photograph by J. A. Hampton

Manchester City captain Roy Paul, with his son Ronald, leaves the pitch at Wembley
after beating Birmingham City 3-1 in the FA Cup Final. May 1956. Photographer not known

Opposite: Birmingham City and Manchester City in the tunnel before kick-off. May 1956.
Photographer not known

The coffin is a prop for a cowboy gunfight staged at
The Den before Millwall's Sixth Round FA Cup tie against
Ipswich Town. March 1978. Photographer not known

Opposite: Queens Park Rangers supporters before
the League Cup Final against West Bromwich Albion.
March 1967. Photographer not known

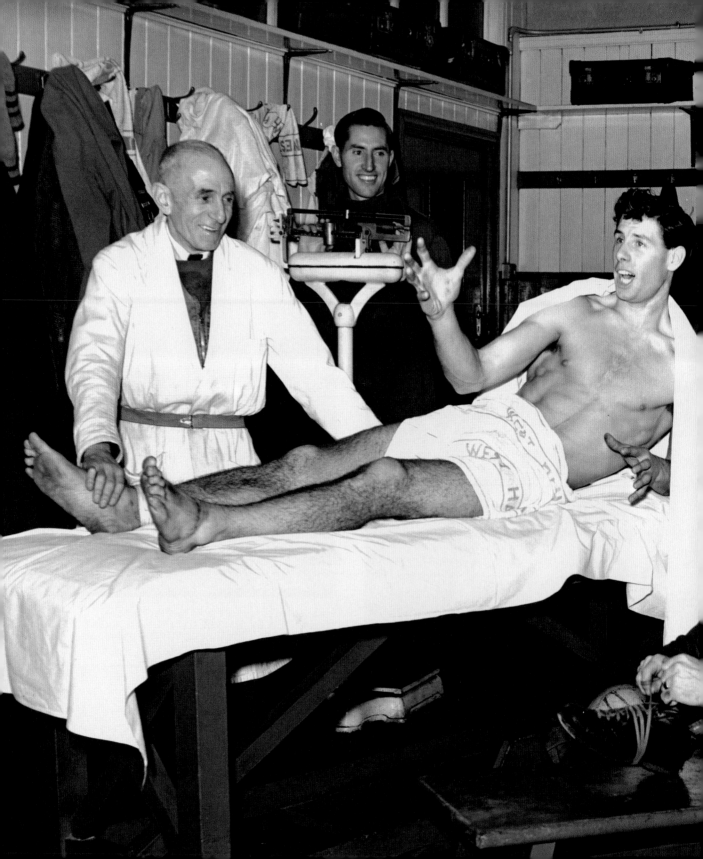

West Ham United's inside-forward Gordon Johnston, a promising light baritone, sings to his team-mates in the treatment room after training. November 1953.
Photographer not known

Bolton Wanderers return home after beating
Manchester City 1–0 in the FA Cup Final. April 1926.
Photographer not known

Bristol Rovers captain Ray Warren looks at the Eastville pitch, which is three feet under water, two days before the Third Round FA Cup tie against Aldershot. January 1951. Photograph by Burchell

Kick-off is delayed at White Hart Lane before the Third Round FA Cup replay between Tottenham Hotspur and Leeds United. January 1954. Photograph by Monty Fresco

Chelsea's Terry Venables marries Christine McCann at
St Cedd's in Canning Town, London. Vicar Robin Bennett
is a West Ham United supporter. April 1966.
Photographer not known

Charlton Athletic supporters at The Valley. January 1938. Photograph by J.A. Hampton

Opposite: Aston Villa supporters before the FA Cup Final against Manchester United.
May 1957. Photographer not known

Patients at Moorfields Eye Hospital, London, listen to a radio broadcast of England versus Scotland. The blackboard shows a grid, devised by the BBC, that helps listeners fix the position of the ball during play; it gave rise to the expression 'back to square one'. April 1932. Photographer not known

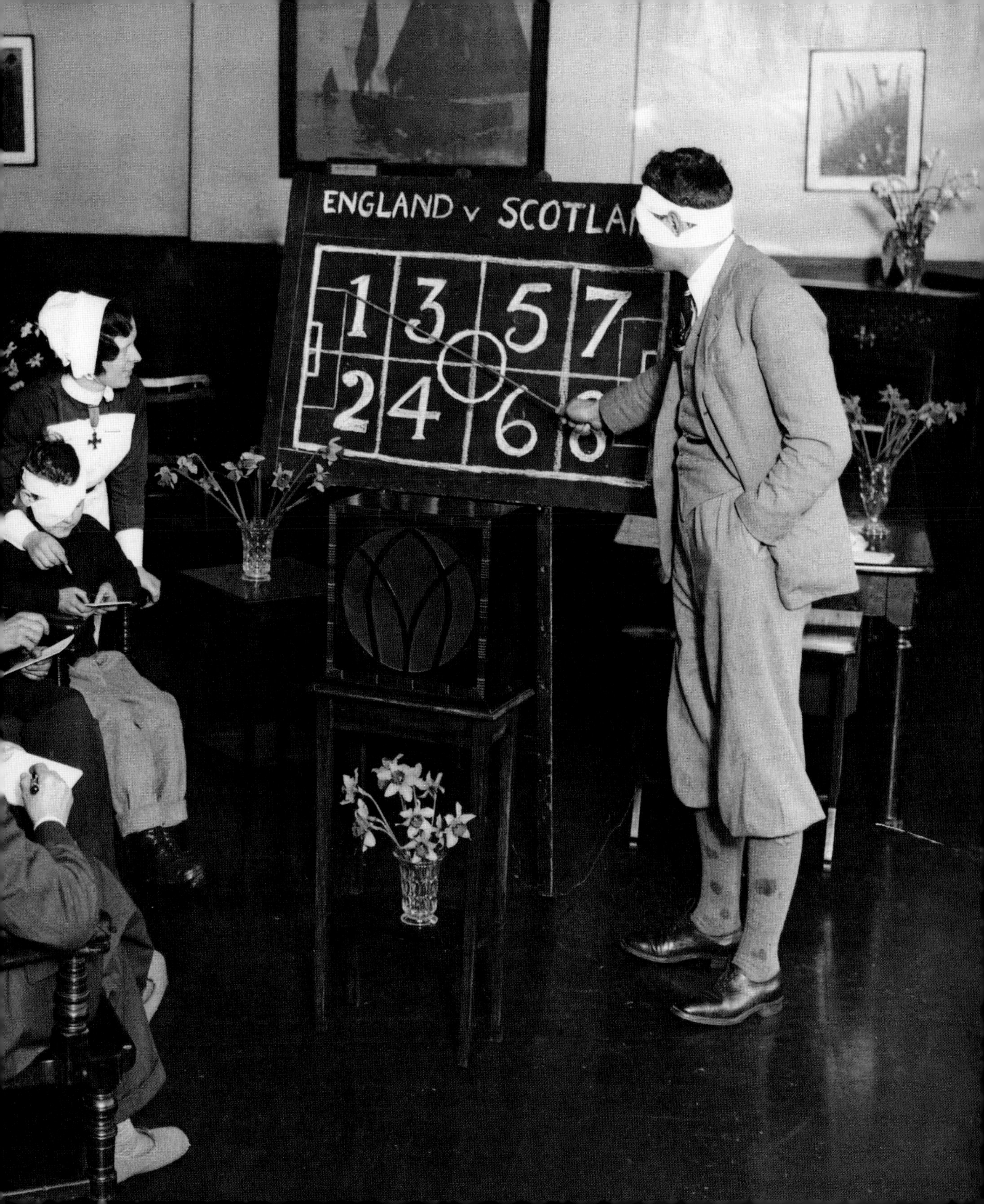
ENGLAND v SCOTLAN
1 3 5 7
2 4 6 8

Everton supporters, in London for the FA Cup Final, encounter Muhammad Ali, in training for his forthcoming fight against Henry Cooper. May 1966.
Photographer not known

Stamford Bridge overflows
when Chelsea play a friendly
against Dynamo Moscow.
November 1945. Photographer
not known

Scotland supporters in Trafalgar Square, London, celebrating the 3–1
Home Championship defeat of England. April 1949. Photograph by J. Waldorf

Opposite: On the way to Wembley, where Scotland draw 1–1 with England.
April 1947. Photograph by John Drysdale

Portsmouth supporters, Fratton Park. December 1951. Photograph by George Douglas

Opposite: Sitting on barriers at The Den. January 1938. Photograph by E. Dean

Arsenal supporters at Kings Cross station on their way to Huddersfield for the FA Cup
Semi-final against Grimsby Town. March 1936. Photograph by E. Dean

Tottenham Hotspur supporters leave Euston station for the Fifth Round FA Cup tie
against Everton. February 1937. Photograph by E. Dean

Mothers and babies queue at the Town Hall for tickets for Gateshead's Sixth Round FA Cup tie against Bolton Wanderers. February 1953. Photograph by Lauder

NOTICE

Admission will be refused to any person found carrying flags, bottles or any other missiles.

Any person found inside the ground in posse⟨⟩ of flags, bottles or a⟨⟩ ⟨m⟩issiles will be re⟨⟩ the premises and ⟨⟩uted.

Instructions ⟨⟩ given to the pol⟨⟩ these measures int⟨⟩

Glasgow Rangers versus Celtic at Ibrox Park. October 1949. Photograph by John Chillingworth

Opposite: Police and players attempt to persuade a supporter to leave the pitch during Crystal Palace's Fourth Round FA Cup tie against Everton at Selhurst Park. January 1931. Photographer not known

A corner shop in Highbury, London. Bertie Mee's Arsenal have just won
the First Division Championship by beating Tottenham Hotspur in the last
game of the season. Days later they complete the double with a 2–1 win
over Liverpool in the FA Cup Final. May 1971. Photographer not known

Opposite: Freida and Frank Hearn wait to board the 'Ipswich Special'
taking Fulham supporters to their Second Round FA Cup tie. January 1957.
Photograph by William Vanderson

Jimmy Greaves in AC Milan's San Siro stadium. Greaves started the 1961 season with AC but – after scoring nine times in 14 games – was playing for Tottenham Hotspur by December of the same year. April 1961. Photograph by Norman Quicke

Opposite: Missing an England training session to rest his shin, which was gashed in the World Cup group game against France. The injury keeps Greaves out of the team and, despite recovering, denies him a place in the Final against West Germany. July 1966. Photographer not known

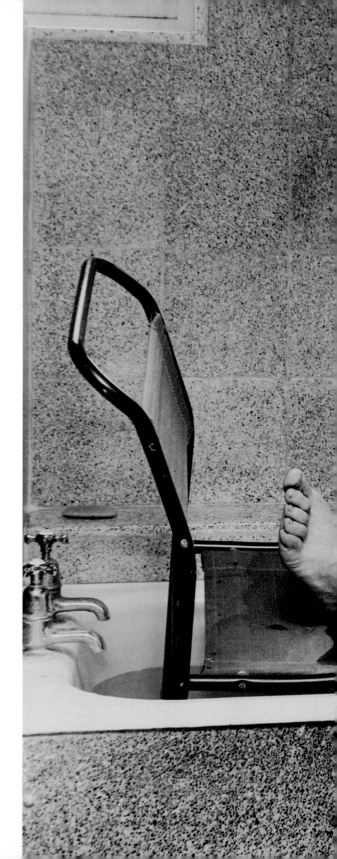

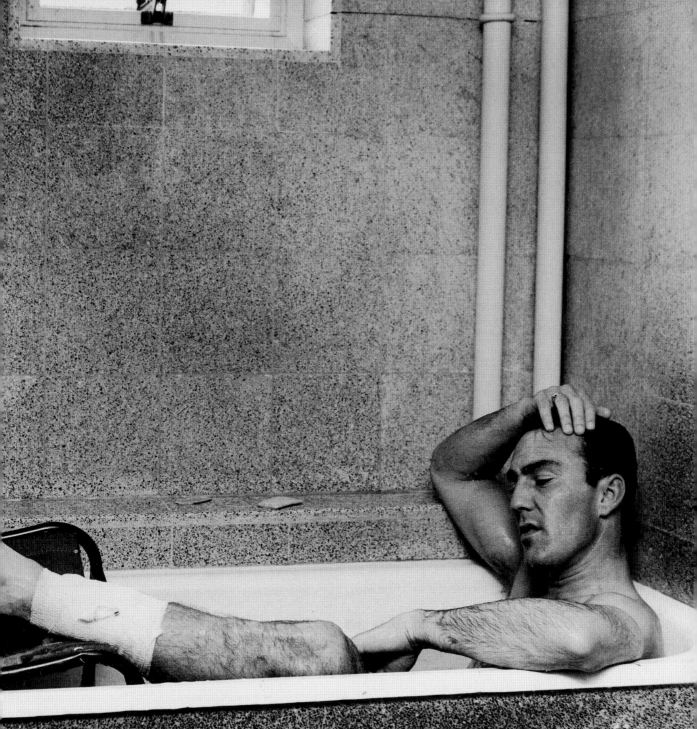

Miss Miller, football coach for Crawley Downs Church School, Surrey, with her squad. September 1931. Photographer not known

Miss Casey coaches the team, who were unbeaten last season, at her school in Bradford. September 1936. Photographer not known

Millwall captain Dave Magnall after his team's 2–0 victory over Manchester City in the Sixth Round of the FA Cup at The Den. March 1937. Photographer not known

Millwall's lion mascot falls over as the team runs out. March 1927. Photograph by H.F. Davis

Opposite: The annual Jockeys versus Variety Artists charity game, to be held this year at Stamford Bridge, is postponed. December 1914. Photographer not known

Stanley Matthews signs autographs before his farewell game – a Stanley Matthews XI versus a World XI – at Stoke City's Victoria Ground. Alongside Matthews are Tony Waiters and Jimmy Armfield (Blackpool); George Cohen and Johnny Haynes (Fulham); Bobby Thompson (Wolverhampton Wanderers); Denis Law and Bobby Charlton (Manchester United); and Jimmy Greaves, Alan Gilzean and Cliff Jones (Tottenham Hotspur). Playing for the World XI are Lev Yashin (Russia); Karl Heinz Schnellinger and Wolfgang Weber (West Germany); Josef Masopust and Jan Popluhar (Czechoslovakia); Jim Baxter and Willie Henderson (Scotland); Raymond Kopa (France); Alfredo di Stefano (Spain); Ferenc Puskas (Hungary); and Eusebio (Portugal). April 1965. Photographer not known

Alf Ramsey with a crystal ball on which are engraved the names of England's World Cup-winning team. September 1966. Photograph by A. Jones

Opposite: At an England training session before a friendly against the USSR. February 1968. Photographer not known

St James's Park before
the FA Cup Quarter-final
against Hull City. March 1930.
Photographer not known

Nat Lofthouse leads Bolton Wanderers up to receive FA Cup winners' medals as the losing Manchester United manager, Matt Busby (in hat), walks away. May 1958. Photographer not known

Opposite: Busby tries out the Wembley pitch on the morning of the European Cup Final against Benfica. May 1968. Photographer not known

Street game, Brindley Road, Notting Hill, London. 1957. Photograph by Roger Mayne

Opposite: Street game, Southam Street, Notting Hill, London. 1956. Photograph by Roger Mayne

England Ladies versus France Ladies. May 1925. Photograph by Edward G. Malindine

Opposite: The Honourable Irene Lawley kicks off a Royal Army Medical Corps match. February 1916. Photographer not known

The wives and girlfriends of the Liverpool squad are in London for the FA Cup Final against Arsenal. May 1971. Photograph by Leonard Burt

Opposite: Ian St John travels back to Liverpool with the FA Cup after scoring the decisive goal in the 2–1 victory over Leeds United in the Final. May 1965. Photographer not known

Newcastle United supporters before their Fifth Round FA Cup tie against Swansea City. February 1952. Photographer not known

Opposite: SS 'Bernicia' takes Newcastle United mascot 'Felix' to London for the FA Cup Final against Aston Villa. April 1924. Photograph by Brooke

Light is so bad in the second half of Charlton Athletic versus Burton Albion that spectators light newspapers to act as flares. January 1956. Photograph by Greaves

Opposite: A Blackpool supporter travels on the overnight 'Special' to London for the 1948 Cup Final against Manchester United. April 1948. Photographer not known

Following pages: Double-winning Tottenham Hotspur's pre-season photo-call at their training ground in Cheshunt, Hertfordhire. August 1961. Photographer not known

Plymouth Argyle trainer Tommy Haynes points the way to promotion, but next season finds them still in Division Three South. August 1926. Photograph by Gill

Opposite: Unidentified goalkeeper practises kicking. 1939. Photographer not known

Bobby and Tina Moore in matching cardigans for 'Woman's Realm'.
October 1965. Photographer not known

Opposite: Modelling for 'Vogue'. September 1962. Photograph by Peter Rand

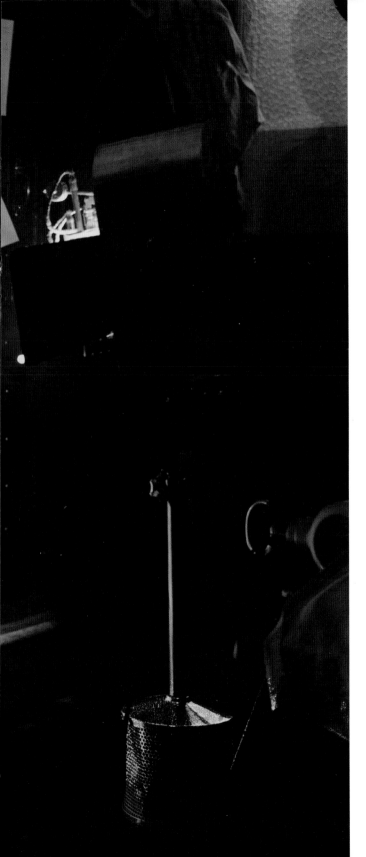

Left to right: right-back Jock Marshall, inside-forward
Jackie Carr and half-back Billy Ellerington of Middlesbrough.
1923. Photographer not known

Opposite: Sunlamp treatment at Highbury. January 1931.
Photographer not known

Jimmy Greaves signs autographs after making his Tottenham Hotspur debut in a reserve game at Plymouth Argyle. December 1961. Photographer not known

Tom Finney, the 'Preston Plumber', at work three months after his first-team debut for Preston North End. His father had advised him to get a trade. November 1946.
Photograph by Charles Hewitt

Opposite: Frank Cotterill, who played for Aston Villa, Southend United and Watford, has become a printer's reel-hand since retiring from the game. February 1932.
Photograph by J.A. Hampton

The England squad on the
day before the World Cup
Final. July 1966. Photograph
by Terry Fincher

Guards at the Tower of London. January 1929. Photographer not known

The Anfield boot-room. Left to right: Roy Evans, reserve team coach; Tom Saunders, European scout; Joe Fagan, assistant manager; Bob Paisley, manager; and Ronnie Moran, chief coach. May 1980. Photograph by John Dawes

Scotland supporters on the Strand, London. April 1947. Photographer not known

Opposite: The Metropolitan Police on duty during the World Cup Finals. July 1966. Photographer not known

Manchester City supporters in Trafalgar Square before the FA Cup Final against Everton. April 1933. Photograph by J.A. Hampton

Opposite: An Everton supporter celebrates the 3–0 FA Cup Final victory over Manchester City in Trafalgar Square. April 1933. Photographer not known

Arsenal manager Tom Whittaker receives a painting, entitled 'Tom Whittaker's Secret', from a Mr A. Warwick of 'John Bull' magazine. On the right is the artist, Yates Wilson, who was originally commissioned by the magazine to paint a front cover. December 1947. Photographer not known

Opposite: The team recreate the scene at Highbury. From left to right: Ronnie Rooke, Leslie Compton, Archie MacAuly, James Logie, Wally Barnes, Reg Lewis, 'Paddy' Sloan, George Hale, Bryn Jones and Denis Compton. December 1947. Photographer not known

Autograph hunters at Highbury. August 1946. Photographer not known

Opposite: Supporters arrive at Wembley to see England versus Hungary. November 1953. Photographer not known

Bobby and Jackie Charlton in their home town of Ashington, Northumberland, after England's World Cup Final victory. August 1966. Photographer not known

Opposite: Bobby Charlton recovers in a Munich hospital after the aircrash that took the lives of eight of his team-mates. February 1958. Photographer not known

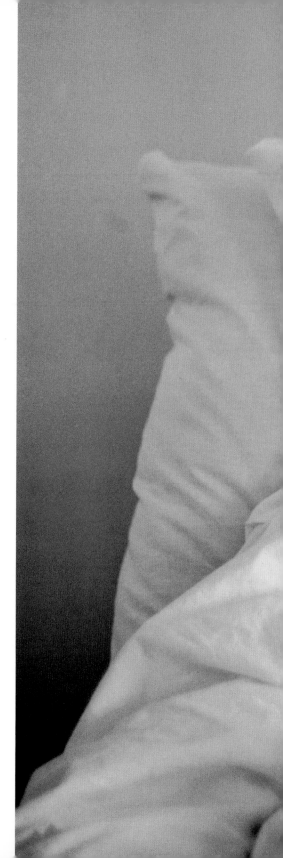

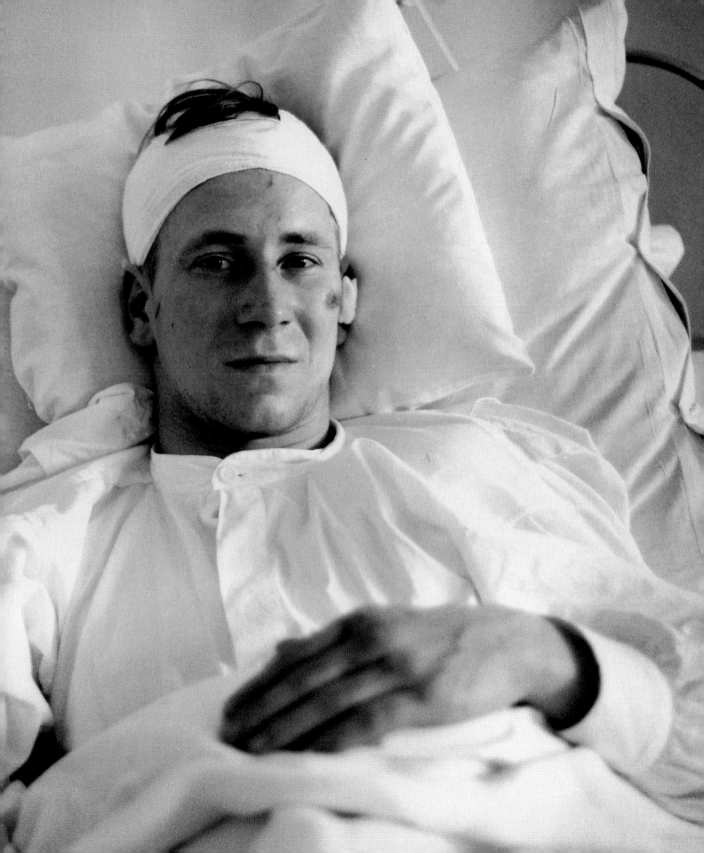

Arsenal versus Tottenham. The North Bank, Highbury.
January 1934. Photograph by A. Hudson

Back row, left to right: Phil Beal, Tottenham Hotspur; Martin Buchan, Manchester United; Malcolm Allison, Manchester City manager; Martin Chivers, Tottenham Hotspur; Gordon Banks, Stoke City; Terry Mancini, Queens Park Rangers. Front row, left to right: Rodney Marsh, Manchester City; Francis Lee, Manchester City; Dave Webb, Chelsea; Geoff Hurst, Stoke City. Allison, 'The Godfather', and his capos meet in a Manchester restaurant. September 1972. Photograph by Terry O'Neill

Opposite: back row, left to right: Alan Ball, Arsenal; Geoff Hurst, West Ham United; Terry Venables, Queens Park Rangers. Front row, left to right: Terry Mancini, Queen's Park Rangers; Dave Webb, Chelsea; Alan Hudson, Chelsea; Rodney Marsh, Queens Park Rangers. They call themselves 'The Clan' and are pictured here at Trattoria Est on London's Fleet Street. March 1972. Photograph by Terry O'Neill

West Bromwich Albion at Paddington station
after beating Birmingham City 2–1 in the FA Cup Final.
April 1931. Photographer not known

Bill Shankly answers fan mail at home in Liverpool. October 1975.
Photograph by John Dawes

Opposite: Following Liverpool's 2–1 defeat of Leeds United in the
FA Cup Final. May 1965. Photograph by Michael Webb

George Best outside Mrs Fullaway's – his digs in Manchester.
1965. Photograph by Ray Green

Opposite: At Manchester United's Cliff training ground in Salford.
1964. Photographer not known

Goalkeeper Jim Sanders looks away as team-mate Ronnie Allen equalises from the penalty spot for West Bromwich Albion in the FA Cup Final against Preston North End. Albion go on to win 3–2. May 1954.
Photographer not known

INDEX

PHOTOGRAPHIC CREDITS
Zelda Cheatle Gallery: 330, 331
Daily Express: 106-107, 172, 209, 227,
232-233, 314, 344, 366, 378-379
Hulton Getty: endpapers, jacket
front, 9, 10-11, 12-13, 16-17, 18, 19,
20-21, 24-25, 26-27, 28, 30-31, 33, 34,
36-37, 40, 40-41, 42-43, 48-49, 50-51,
51, 52-53, 54, 55, 56, 56-57, 60, 60-61,
62-63, 64, 66-67, 68, 72-73, 73, 74, 75,
77, 80-81, 88-89, 90, 90-91, 92, 93,
94-95, 98, 99, 100-101, 102, 110, 113,
114-115, 116, 117, 118, 118-119, 120-
121, 121, 122-123, 126-127, 128, 130-
131, 132, 132-133, 134-135, 135, 136,
137, 138, 140, 142-143, 147, 148-149,
154-155, 157, 158-159, 160-161, 161,
163, 166, 167, 168-169, 170, 170-171,
174-175, 176-177, 178, 179, 180-181,
182-183, 188-189, 189, 190-191, 192-
193, 194-195, 196, 199, 200, 202-203,
206-207, 208-209, 210, 211, 214, 215,
218, 222, 224-225, 228-229, 230, 240,
242-243, 246, 247, 248-249, 252-253,
253, 256-257, 258, 259, 260-261, 261,
262, 263, 264-265, 266-267, 270, 271,
272, 273, 274, 275, 276-277, 278-279,
280-281, 285, 288-289, 290, 291, 292-
293, 294, 296-297, 302-303, 304, 305,
306, 307, 310, 312, 313, 316, 317, 318-
319, 320, 321, 322-323, 324, 326-327,
332-333, 333, 334, 336-337, 337, 342,
343, 346-347, 347, 350, 350-351, 352-
353, 354-355, 358, 359, 360, 361, 364,
366-367, 368-369, 374-375
Littlewoods Pools: 44, 45
Popperfoto: jacket back, 14-15, 24, 29,
32, 38-39, 46-47, 65, 68-69, 71, 82-83,
84, 85, 86, 96-97, 103, 104-105, 105,
108, 109, 110-111, 159, 164-165, 173,
186, 187, 196-197, 219, 223, 226, 231,
238, 239, 244-245, 245, 265, 282, 283,
286-287, 295, 298-299, 300-301, 303,
310-311, 328, 328-329, 338, 340-341,
362, 362-363, 372-373, 376, 377
Private collection: 356-357
Science & Society Picture Library: 22,
70, 76, 78, 79, 112, 140-141, 144-145,
150, 184, 184-185, 198, 216-217, 220-
221, 241, 250, 251, 254-255, 268-269,
308-309, 325, 334-335, 339, 365, 374
Terry O'Neill: 212-213, 370, 371
Topham Picturepoint: 23, 34-35, 58,
59, 86-87, 124-125, 129, 139, 142, 146-
147, 151, 152-153, 156, 162-163, 200-
201, 204-205, 234-235, 236-237, 249,
284-285, 314-315, 345, 348-349

Cassell & Co acknowledge the
assistance provided by Charles
Merullo and colleagues in the
Publishing Projects Department at
Getty Images/Hulton Getty.

Hulton|Archive

ACKNOWLEDGEMENTS

**For Julie,
United Forever...**

My special thanks are due to
Steve Guise, Colin Jacobson and Jack Tennant who
contributed enormously to this project.

My thanks also to old and new friends for their patience, support and expertise:

Alan Ashby, Marcel Ashby, Neil Burgess, Gordon Burn,
Patrick Carpenter, Zelda Cheatle, Sue Cranmer, Clive Crook,
Nick Culpeper, Mark Debnam, Stuart Dempster, Tony Eyles,
Terry Fincher, Mike Freeman, Nick Goater, David Godwin,
Paul Goodman, Carol Gorner, Brendan and Deborah Hayes,
Suzanne Hodgart, Justin Hunt, Penny Jones, Shem Law,
Margaret Little, Rodney Marsh, Roger Mayne, Caroline Metcalfe,
John Mitchinson, Chris Myers, Amanda Nevill, Terry O'Neill,
Michael Rand, David Robson, Don Stick, Alice Tennant,
Jamie Trendall, Louise Walker, Adam Ward, Jon Waters.
And my Mum and Dad, of course, for that 1963 Cup Final ticket...

Picture sources:

Phil Burnham-Richards, Joelle Ferly, Charles Merullo and Liz Ihre at Hulton Getty,
Brian Liddy and Anne Bucktrout at the National Museum of Photography, Film & Television,
Angela Murphy and Venita Paul at Science & Society Picture Library,
Liz Pendleton at Littlewoods Pools,
Alan Smith and Mark Dowd at Topham Picturepoint,
Andrew Wrighting, Sylvia Duffin and David Upton at Popperfoto.

All Football clubs and organisations who helped with caption detail, particularly:

David Barber at the Football Association, Ian Cook at Arsenal,
Peter Hall at Plymouth Argyle, Graham Hughes at Wolverhampton Wanderers,
Phil Noble at Manchester City, Andy Porter and John Rayner at Tottenham Hotspur,
Peter Stewart at West Ham, Richard Walker at Watford, Ted Wilding at Millwall.

... and Bruce Bernard.